INTRODUCTION

This book introduces four types of martial art – judo, tae kwon do, tai chi, and karate. *Martial arts* might seem like an unusual term for these activities because martial means warlike. However, although most of the martial arts mentioned here originated as combat or fighting skills, the people featured in this book practise their martial arts in order to develop confidence, fitness, and self-defence skills.*

All of the martial arts featured in this book began in Asia, and although they are now practised all around the world, many of the customs and the traditional words and phrases that relate to each discipline are still an important part of the training. Many martial arts have ranking or grading systems that are conveyed by different-coloured belts. The colours used can vary according to the art, school, and instructor.

*Please note that you should not attempt the techniques described in this book unless a qualified instructor is present.

1. JUDO

Interview with Anjuli

Why did you decide to start judo?

I did a modelling course once, and we were talking about self-defence, and the teacher said that judo was good for that. I had a friend who was already doing it, and she told me to come along and watch. So I did, and it looked like fun.

And is judo good for self-defence?

It's really good because it's all about being able to wrestle someone to the ground. So if someone grabbed me, I'd be able to throw them. Well, that's the idea, anyway.

Do you think that you could throw someone if you had to?

Maybe. I'm not totally confident that I could, but I'm much more likely to be able to because I've done judo.

"I'm an orange belt with a green to

MARTIAL ARTS

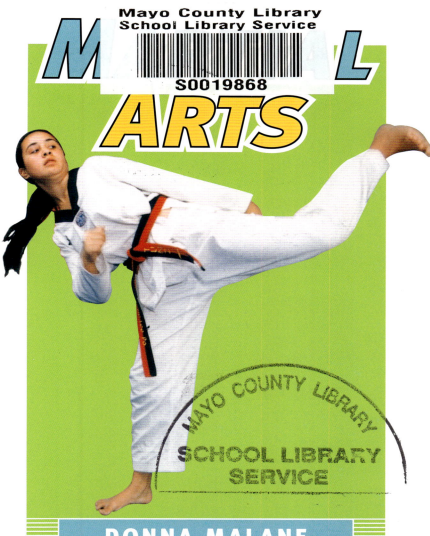

DONNA MALANE
photographs by Mark Coote

CONTENTS

What do you like best about judo?

I like all of it, especially the throws. I like the way you have to really earn your grades. They don't just get given to you. You have to work hard for them, and I like that.

What grade are you at now?

I'm an orange belt with a green tab. That's taken me just over a year to get.

How do you get graded?

You have to do sets of throws and falls, and the teacher watches and marks you. You find out later if you've passed or not.

How often do you train?

Only once a week at the **dojo,** but I practise a bit on my sister.

What would you say to someone thinking of starting judo?

I'd tell them to go along and watch first, and if they think it looks like fun, then they should join.

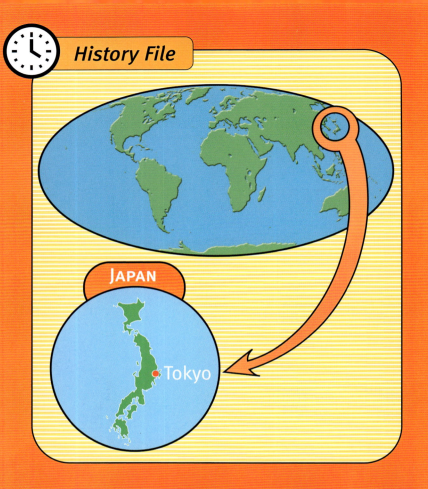

JAPAN

Tokyo

Modern judo was
founded in 1882 by
Professor Jigoro
Kano of Japan.

1860 1870 1880 1890 1900 1910 192

One of the first things taught in judo is how to balance. In judo competitions, each person fights or wrestles with an opponent. The aim is to unbalance your opponent and then to throw or trip them down onto the mat and hold them there. You can only throw someone if you are totally balanced.

The first World Judo Championships were held in Tokyo in 1956.

Judo became an Olympic sport in 1964.

930   1940   1950   1960   1970   1980   1990   2000

The three main types of move are:

1. Breakfalls

When a **judoka** falls or is thrown on
the mat, they must land
in such a way that they
don't get hurt. To do
this, they must roll and
slap the mat with their arm and
the palm of their hand to take the full
force of the fall.

2. Throws

There are sixty-five types of judo throw. They
allow someone to throw their opponent forwards,
backwards, and to the side. The person who
makes the throw is called the **tori**, and the
person being thrown is the **uke**.

3. Groundwork

This includes all of the judo moves that are performed while opponents are lying on the mat. A **hold-down** is a groundwork technique where the opponent is pinned on their back and held down for 30 seconds.

Judo Belt Colours

White ⋯⋯▷ Yellow ⋯⋯▷ Orange

Green ⋯⋯▷ Blue ⋯⋯▷ Brown ⋯⋯▷ Black

? Did You Know?

The introduction of weight categories, which meant that people competed in a grade according to their body weight, greatly influenced the development of judo as a sport because it encouraged the participation of women and junior competitors.

The first women's World Judo Championships were held in New York in 1980, and Junior World Championship competitions have been held since 1976.

Words Relating to Judo

(These words are printed in bold type the first time they appear in the book.)

dojo: a hall or room where judo is practised
hold-down: holding your opponent down on their back for a set time
judo: the gentle way
judoka: a person who practises judo
tori: the person who throws
uke: the person being thrown

2. TAE KWON DO

Interview with Stevie-Lee

Why did you decide to learn tae kwon do?
My older sister started first, then I joined, then my two little brothers. My cousins do it as well, so I guess it's a family thing. Even my dad does tae kwon do now.

What level are you at now?
I'm a black belt 1st **dan**.

You're a black belt! How old are you?
I'm actually a junior black belt because you're not allowed to be a full black belt until you're fifteen. I'm only thirteen. My sister is fifteen, and she's already a full black belt 2nd dan.

66 *I'm a black belt 1st dan.* 99

Has your attitude to tae kwon do changed since you started?

Yeah. I've been doing it for three or four years now. It's harder to get motivated now.

Why is that?

I guess because as your rank gets higher, the training gets more difficult. I practise twice a week for an hour and a half each session and more often when there's a tournament coming up.

Did you think, when you started, that you would get this far?

I didn't think that I'd get to black belt, but I'm really pleased that I have. I wasn't very fit when I started, but I am now. Getting really fit is one of the best things about tae kwon do.

Do you think of tae kwon do as a fighting skill or a self-defence skill?

In a tournament, you do fight, but you wear full-body padding, and there are rules about where you can't kick, for example, to the face. I've never had to use tae kwon do to defend myself in the street, but it really boosts your confidence, knowing that you have this thing – this ability to protect yourself.

Do your friends try to get you to fight them?

To be honest, my friends aren't that interested. Anyhow, there are strict rules about using tae kwon do techniques outside the **do jang**. You can get expelled from the club if you use tae kwon do against someone, unless you're defending yourself.

What would you say to someone who was thinking of taking up tae kwon do?

I would definitely tell them to join.

Fact File

Tae kwon do is a method of self-defence that uses the hands and feet. It is often known as "the way of the hand and foot".

There are three aspects to tae kwon do: the *body*, the *mind*, and the *spirit*, and if all three aren't part of the learning, then a student won't have a complete understanding of tae kwon do.

History File

- Tae kwon do began in Korea about 2000 years ago.
- United States servicemen returning from Korea introduced tae kwon do into the United States in the 1950s.
- Tae kwon do was accepted as an Olympic sport in 1988.

KOREA

North Korea

●Seoul

South Korea

The moves are similar to those used in karate, but the feet are used more in tae kwon do.

Eighty percent of the moves are done with the foot (kicks), and twenty percent are done with the hand (strikes).

The moves also involve stances (the way a person stands), blocks, breathing, rhythm, and balance.

There are two styles of tae kwon do – the International Taekwondo Federation (ITF) and the World or Olympic Taekwondo Federation (WTF). The WTF rules allow for full-impact hits and kicks to the head and body and demand a high level of fitness. Full-body padding is used in WTF tournament matches.

Tae Kwon Do Belt Colours

White ⋯⋗ Yellow ⋯⋗ Green ⋯⋗ Blue ⋯⋗ Red ⋯⋗ Black

Words Relating to Tae Kwon Do

dan: the advanced grade for black belts

do jang: the hall or room where tae kwon do is practised

tae kwon do:

    tae jumping or flying

    kwon to use the force of the fist

    do the art or the way of

3. TAI CHI

Interview with Jack

Why did you decide to do tai chi?
I've always wanted to do tai chi because I've seen people in the park doing it, and the way they moved together looked really cool.

Now that you've done your first tai chi lesson, was it how you imagined it would be?
Yes. The first twenty minutes was cool, the second twenty minutes was a bit harder, then the last twenty minutes – I was really lost!

Why? Did it get more difficult?
You get really aware of your body and how it all fits together. And then you have to just move one bit of it, and ... I don't know ... it's kind of weird, because it looks really easy to do, but it's not.

first time at tai chi ...

Do you think it would be easier if you were really fit?
No, I don't. I think it's about balance and breathing and stuff. I'm sure I'd get better if I kept on doing it.

How did you feel while you were doing it?
I felt a bit stupid because everyone else in the class had been doing it for a while and this was my first lesson, but nobody seemed to notice me or stare at me or anything.

How did your body feel afterwards?
That was really strange because, even when I walked out of the lesson, I felt like I was moving differently. Like I said, tai chi makes you really aware of your body and how it moves and how you breathe.

You focus on your body?

Yeah, that's it exactly. I could feel how locked up my body had got from sitting down at school all day, and I spend a lot of time at my computer. Doing tai chi kind of unlocked me.

What would you say to someone thinking of doing tai chi?

I'd say if you want to do a martial art but you don't want to do kung fu fighting and kicking, then tai chi is a great thing to do.

Fact File

Tai chi is practised for different reasons. Some people do it for exercise and to keep healthy. Other people believe that tai chi is a way to gain a better understanding of life.

One of the best things about tai chi is that once a student has learned the moves, they can practise it almost anywhere, any time, and on their own if they want. The moves are aimed at allowing the body's **ji** to flow.

Tai chi is a set of slow, graceful moves made in a continuous, flowing sequence. Although it might look easy, it's very difficult to do really well. Even people who have been practising tai chi for many years say that they are still working towards improving their movements.

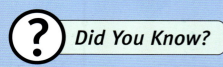

? Did You Know?

There are 44 to 108 movements in tai chi, depending on the style being learnt. The movements include:

- Grasp the bird's tail
- White crane spreads wings
- Needle at the bottom of the sea
- Cloud arms
- Carry tiger to mountain
- Wild horse parts mane

🕐 *History File*

Tai chi was founded about 800 years ago by Zhang San Feng, who lived on Wudang mountain in Huipei province, China. However, the teaching and practice of tai chi did not become widespread in China until the nineteenth century. Today tai chi is popular with people all around the world.

CHINA

Wudang ●

Words Relating to Tai Chi

ji: energy or spirit
tai chi: grand, ultimate fist

4. KARATE

What was it like when you first started learning karate?

Really weird. For ages, everyone was so much better at it than I was, but I've been doing karate now for about a year, so that seems ages ago now.

In what way is karate different from how you thought it would be?

I thought there would be lots of hitting and punching and stuff, but there's much more to it than that. There are sets of movements called **katas**, which are like moves in a sequence that you have to learn. They're cool.

I've been doing karate now for about a year.

How fit do you have to be to do karate?

You don't have to be super-fit, but you do get fit doing it. I feel really hyped when I start a class.

Have you ever been hurt during karate training?

Once when I was going through some set moves. I was blocking and punching, and I drove my shin into this guy's elbow. I got lots of bruises, but bruising is a good sign, actually, because it shows that your tissue is healing.

Why do you yell out when you make a karate move?

That's called **kiai**. It sounds like a Jackie Chan film, doesn't it? A really powerful kiai can have a shock-wave effect on the person you're up against. It's also supposed to frighten them and at the same time give you courage. It's kind of a mix between the sound a weightlifter makes when they lift weights and the sound of a battle-cry to scare the other person silly.

What about the bowing – what's that all about?
You bow as a symbol of respect, that's all. You don't bow, like, to say I'm lower than that person or anything. There's this saying in seido karate that you can't respect others unless you respect yourself first, and being able to bow to someone without getting all embarrassed and stuff is part of that. It feels a bit weird at first, but you get used to it.

Has doing karate made you want to fight with people at school?
No, karate isn't like that at all. It does the opposite because I feel more confident, so I don't need to prove anything.

Have you ever used karate to defend yourself?
No, but last summer I was playing cricket, and a boy threw a ball at another kid's head, and I just reached out and grabbed the ball! I'd moved so fast, I even surprised myself! My reflexes were really sharp, and I'm sure that's from doing karate. It felt good.

What would you say to someone thinking of taking up karate?
Do it!

There are many different styles of karate, or **karate do**, which is the proper name for karate. Hunter practises seido karate. The head of seido karate is Kaicho Tadashi Nakamura, who lives in New York.

People who practise seido karate wear the Nakamura family emblem on the sleeve of their **gi**. The three circles inside the flower petal stand for love, respect, and obedience, which is the motto for seido karate.

History File

Karate originated in Okinawa, a Japanese island lying between Japan and China. In the seventeenth century, the Okinawan people were banned from carrying weapons. The Chinese soldiers who were living on the island at this time practised karate. The Okinawan people studied the karate techniques and learnt ways of protecting themselves without weapons.

Karate was introduced into the mainland of Japan about 100 years ago and is now one of the most popular martial arts in the world.

Karate Moves

1. Making a fist

The thumb must always be held
outside the fingers when
making a fist. If the
thumb is closed inside
the fist, it could get broken.

2. Blocking

Blocking is an important karate technique. It is
a defensive move to avoid being hit.

3. Kicking

Karate moves are made up of punches, blocks, and kicks. It is important that a person protects their toes when performing a kick, or they could hurt themselves badly.

Karate Belt Colours

White ····▷ Blue ····▷ Yellow

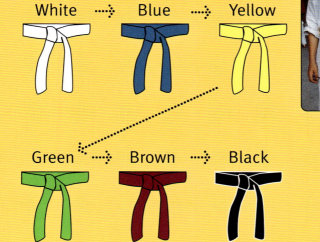

Green ····▷ Brown ····▷ Black

? Did You Know?

A popular image of karate is people breaking bricks and concrete with their bare hands. This technique, known as atemi waza, can result in injury unless it is taught properly.

Karate is often perceived as being violent and aggressive, but, in fact, it teaches self-control, respect, and confidence.

Words Relating to Karate

dojo:	the training hall where karate is practised
gi:	the white suit worn at practice
juku:	a special or unique place
karate do:	the way of the empty hand
karateka:	people who practise karate
kata:	a set of moves
kiai:	the loud yell or shout made during the moves

FINDING OUT MORE ABOUT MARTIAL ARTS

- Check out the library for books on martial arts.

- Search the Internet. You could try the following keywords: "martial arts" followed by the martial art you are interested in, for example, "karate".

- Ask around. Find someone who is learning a martial art and ask if you can go and watch a class.

- Visit or phone a martial arts shop. They often have noticeboards that advertise classes. Ask the people who work at the shop to recommend a class.

- If you find an instructor or a class, make sure that they are registered with a national or international martial arts organisation.

INDEX